90 DAY
DEVOTIONAL
JOURNAL

"You are blessed MORE than you think!"

DR. MARVIN T. PREVOST

EXTREME SUCCESS: 90 DAY DEVOTIONAL JOURNAL

Copyright © 2019 Marvin T. Prevost

Cover Design: C Marcel Wiggins

Dekan Press by MIGMIR All rights reserved. No part of this publication may be reproduced, distributed or transmitted in any form or by any means, without prior written permission. Unless otherwise identified, scripture quotations are from the King James Version of the Bible.

Published by MIGMIR Company USA, LLC

www.migmir.us

For Worldwide Distribution
Printed in the U.S.A.

ISBN: 9780997347777

Library of Congress Control Number: 2019951487

CONTENTS

Acknowledgments 4

Introduction 5

Section 1: Declaring victory in faith over everything 6
    [Days 1-30]

Section 2: Becoming a bolder you! 70
    [Days 31-60]

Section 3: Make the decision: Prepare for the MOVE!......132
    [Days 61-90]

ACKNOWLEDGMENTS

To my wife, Wyetha: Thank you for inspiring me to write this devotional.

This project is also dedicated to my three children, Thomas, Kyle and Zoe, and also to Roman Prevost, (my first grandson) I love you all very much!

INTRODUCTION

The following journal was designed for you in this season of your life and ministry. Most of the days were originally written for social media posts, however God has led me to put them into a journal just for you. Be prepared to be challenged, changed, and catapulted into what God has for you as His Spirit makes His way into the very nooks and crannies of your life for the next 90 days.

It's time to let the enemy know that your time is here, and your time is now! He is preparing a table before you, even now, in the presence of your enemies according to Psalm 23:5.

James 2:17

"Even so faith, if it hath not works, is dead, being alone"!

Lets begin!

Things you may need: (1) Sticky Notes, (2) your faith, (3) the Word of God, and (4) a sense of humor.

SECTION 1

DAYS 1 - 30
Declaring victory in faith over everything!

EXTREME THOUGHT: DAY 1

You! Pick yourself UP. Shake OFF any disappointments. Forget PAST hurts, be free from your failures, and let go of NEGATIVE PEOPLE!

(Now do this physically, "Turn around NOW, WALK in a different direction in your house and yell, I'm free in JESUS!)

What thoughts come to mind when you read the above statement?

_____
_____
_____
_____
_____
_____
_____

Where are you today? Are you successful in this? Why or why not?

_____
_____
_____
_____
_____
_____
_____

Extreme Success: 90 DAY Devotional Journal

What is blocking your success in achieving this?

_____
_____
_____
_____
_____
_____
_____

Consider one or two steps of implementing your success:

_____
_____
_____
_____
_____
_____
_____

Find scriptures to support your success today:

_____
_____
_____
_____
_____
_____
_____

EXTREME THOUGHT: DAY 2

To become strong in the Lord, drink the sincere milk of the Word. Add three daily prayers, subtract sin, multiply your faith, and rightly divide the Word of Truth! BOOM! You are STRONG!

(Now flex your muscles as a reminder that you are strong.)

What thoughts come to mind when you read the above statement?

_____
_____
_____
_____
_____
_____
_____

Where are you today? Are you successful in this? Why or why not?

_____
_____
_____
_____
_____
_____
_____

Extreme Success: 90 DAY Devotional Journal

What is blocking your success in achieving this?

_____
_____
_____
_____
_____
_____
_____

Consider one or two steps of implementing your success:

_____
_____
_____
_____
_____
_____
_____

Find scriptures to support your success today:

_____
_____
_____
_____
_____
_____
_____

EXTREME THOUGHT: DAY 3

When the enemy starts speaking lies into your ears... perform "spiritual surgery" and "cut out his voice box". Stop listening when he speaks as though he has no voice at all.

(Say out loud, "I CAN'T HEAR YOU"!)

What thoughts come to mind when you read the above statement?

_____
_____
_____
_____
_____
_____
_____

Where are you today? Are you successful in this? Why or why not?

_____
_____
_____
_____
_____
_____
_____

Extreme Success: 90 DAY Devotional Journal

What is blocking your success in achieving this?

_____
_____
_____
_____
_____
_____
_____

Consider one or two steps of implementing your success:

_____
_____
_____
_____
_____
_____
_____

Find scriptures to support your success today:

_____
_____
_____
_____
_____
_____
_____

EXTREME THOUGHT: DAY 4

God's plan will happen for you. Your fight is so great because your ministry is so great. If you can fight and sustain in the natural, you will be able to fight and sustain in the spirit. Keep moving through the pain.

(Now walk through your house and say, "keep moving".)

What thoughts come to mind when you read the above statement?

_____
_____
_____
_____
_____
_____
_____

Where are you today? Are you successful in this? Why or why not?

_____
_____
_____
_____
_____
_____
_____

Extreme Success: 90 DAY Devotional Journal

What is blocking your success in achieving this?

_____
_____
_____
_____
_____
_____
_____

Consider one or two steps of implementing your success:

_____
_____
_____
_____
_____
_____
_____

Find scriptures to support your success today:

_____
_____
_____
_____
_____
_____
_____

EXTREME THOUGHT: DAY 5

You can BELIEVE IT! You are guilty as charged. What's being said about you is really you! Don't deny it! You are blessed beyond measure, great, and abundantly!

(Now say out loud, "I am GUILTY"!)

What thoughts come to mind when you read the above statement?

_____
_____
_____
_____
_____
_____
_____

Where are you today? Are you successful in this? Why or why not?

_____
_____
_____
_____
_____
_____
_____

Extreme Success: 90 DAY Devotional Journal

What is blocking your success in achieving this?

_____
_____
_____
_____
_____
_____
_____

Consider one or two steps of implementing your success:

_____
_____
_____
_____
_____
_____
_____

Find scriptures to support your success today:

_____
_____
_____
_____
_____
_____
_____

EXTREME THOUGHT: DAY 6

You got this! It's yours because God planned it! He's giving you the desires of your heart because your desire is in Him. It's manifesting and you will be in full operation with it. It's going to be life changing.

(Say out loud, "I receive it"!)

What thoughts come to mind when you read the above statement?

_____
_____
_____
_____
_____
_____

Where are you today? Are you successful in this? Why or why not?

_____
_____
_____
_____
_____
_____

Extreme Success: 90 DAY Devotional Journal

What is blocking your success in achieving this?

_____
_____
_____
_____
_____
_____
_____

Consider one or two steps of implementing your success:

_____
_____
_____
_____
_____
_____
_____

Find scriptures to support your success today:

_____
_____
_____
_____
_____
_____
_____

EXTREME THOUGHT: DAY 7

Your victory is greater than your defeat! You are an overcomer and not a weakling! You are a conqueror and not a failure! You are a warrior and not a coward! GREAT IS GOD WHO IS IN YOU.

(Write on a piece of paper and post it on your refrigerator "I am an awesome devil chaser".)

What thoughts come to mind when you read the above statement?

_____
_____
_____
_____
_____
_____
_____

Where are you today? Are you successful in this? Why or why not?

_____
_____
_____
_____
_____
_____
_____

Extreme Success: 90 DAY Devotional Journal

What is blocking your success in achieving this?

_____
_____
_____
_____
_____
_____
_____

Consider one or two steps of implementing your success:

_____
_____
_____
_____
_____
_____
_____

Find scriptures to support your success today:

_____
_____
_____
_____
_____
_____
_____

EXTREME THOUGHT: DAY 8

It's your break-out season! Jesus is removing you from that which is frustrating you most. You're stepping out of it! No more! It's done! It's over!

(Now text five people and tell them, "You are coming out of this situation; you are winning".)

What thoughts come to mind when you read the above statement?

_____
_____
_____
_____
_____
_____
_____

Where are you today? Are you successful in this? Why or why not?

_____
_____
_____
_____
_____
_____
_____

Extreme Success: 90 DAY Devotional Journal

What is blocking your success in achieving this?

_____
_____
_____
_____
_____
_____
_____

Consider one or two steps of implementing your success:

_____
_____
_____
_____
_____
_____
_____

Find scriptures to support your success today:

_____
_____
_____
_____
_____
_____
_____

EXTREME THOUGHT: DAY 9

The enemy is always reminding you of who you use to be. God reminds you this day who and whose you are. Simply believe Him.

(Now email three people and say, "simply believe Him".)

What thoughts come to mind when you read the above statement?

_____
_____
_____
_____
_____
_____
_____

Where are you today? Are you successful in this? Why or why not?

_____
_____
_____
_____
_____
_____

Extreme Success: 90 DAY Devotional Journal

What is blocking your success in achieving this?

Consider one or two steps of implementing your success:

Find scriptures to support your success today:

EXTREME THOUGHT: DAY 10

When the enemy says "NO", God says "YES"! God's YES is LOUDER than the enemy's No! You must say "YES" to the enemy when he says No!

(Now say out loud, "Yes! Yes! Yes!")

What thoughts come to mind when you read the above statement?

_____
_____
_____
_____
_____
_____
_____

Where are you today? Are you successful in this? Why or why not?

_____
_____
_____
_____
_____
_____
_____

Extreme Success: 90 DAY Devotional Journal

What is blocking your success in achieving this?

_____
_____
_____
_____
_____
_____
_____

Consider one or two steps of implementing your success:

_____
_____
_____
_____
_____
_____
_____

Find scriptures to support your success today:

_____
_____
_____
_____
_____
_____
_____

EXTREME THOUGHT: DAY 11

What the enemy has been using against you is only going to MAKE YOU. (Laugh at the enemy and say out loud three times, "sticks and stones may break my bones but your accusations will never destroy me.")

What thoughts come to mind when you read the above statement?

Where are you today? Are you successful in this? Why or why not?

Extreme Success: 90 DAY Devotional Journal

What is blocking your success in achieving this?

_____
_____
_____
_____
_____
_____
_____

Consider one or two steps of implementing your success:

_____
_____
_____
_____
_____
_____
_____

Find scriptures to support your success today:

_____
_____
_____
_____
_____
_____
_____

EXTREME THOUGHT: DAY 12

Starting now – it's going to be a season of unexpected & unusual favor, promotions in ministry, enhancements to your calling, gifts instilled and activated in you. You are a powerhouse in God.

(Write this on a piece of paper and say it out loud, "I am a powerhouse in God".)

What thoughts come to mind when you read the above statement?

_____
_____
_____
_____
_____
_____
_____
_____

Where are you today? Are you successful in this? Why or why not?

_____
_____
_____
_____
_____
_____
_____

Extreme Success: 90 DAY Devotional Journal

What is blocking your success in achieving this?

_____
_____
_____
_____
_____
_____
_____

Consider one or two steps of implementing your success:

_____
_____
_____
_____
_____
_____
_____

Find scriptures to support your success today:

_____
_____
_____
_____
_____
_____
_____

EXTREME THOUGHT: DAY 13

Your blessings are about to overtake, consume, and swallow you up like a tidal wave. Your waves of blessings will be constant! Wave after wave.

(Draw on a piece of paper tidal waves getting bigger and bigger. Then Say out loud, "Send your waves Jesus".)

What thoughts come to mind when you read the above statement?

_____
_____
_____
_____
_____
_____
_____

Where are you today? Are you successful in this? Why or why not?

_____
_____
_____
_____
_____
_____
_____

Extreme Success: 90 DAY Devotional Journal

What is blocking your success in achieving this?

_____
_____
_____
_____
_____
_____
_____

Consider one or two steps of implementing your success:

_____
_____
_____
_____
_____
_____
_____

Find scriptures to support your success today:

_____
_____
_____
_____
_____
_____
_____

EXTREME THOUGHT: DAY 14

Go on and give up, throw in the towel, stop battling, end it and say out loud, "Forget it, I'm done. I'm tired of fighting." This is what God's been waiting for you to say. Now give in to Him.

(Go to your bathroom and get a towel. Throw it on the floor and say out loud, "forget it, I'm done. I'm tired of fighting".)

What thoughts come to mind when you read the above statement?

_____
_____
_____
_____
_____
_____

Where are you today? Are you successful in this? Why or why not?

_____
_____
_____
_____
_____
_____
_____

Extreme Success: 90 DAY Devotional Journal

What is blocking your success in achieving this?

_____
_____
_____
_____
_____
_____
_____

Consider one or two steps of implementing your success:

_____
_____
_____
_____
_____
_____
_____

Find scriptures to support your success today:

_____
_____
_____
_____
_____
_____
_____

EXTREME THOUGHT: DAY 15

Jesus is searching for your obedience. Why wait? God has spoken it! Step out into the deep. YOU WON'T DROWN! Even if you sink, YOUR LIFE JACKET is on! Step, step, step out into the deep!

(Now go put on any jacket to remind you of what God said.)

What thoughts come to mind when you read the above statement?

_____
_____
_____
_____
_____
_____
_____

Where are you today? Are you successful in this? Why or why not?

_____
_____
_____
_____
_____
_____
_____

Extreme Success: 90 DAY Devotional Journal

What is blocking your success in achieving this?

_____
_____
_____
_____
_____
_____
_____

Consider one or two steps of implementing your success:

_____
_____
_____
_____
_____
_____
_____

Find scriptures to support your success today:

_____
_____
_____
_____
_____
_____
_____

EXTREME THOUGHT: DAY 16

The glory of God in your life isn't dependent upon people's opinions, thoughts, attitudes, comments, discernments or their anointing! The glory, the oil, the anointing is given by Jesus!

(Call your best friend and only say to them, "I'm confident in myself because of Jesus". Then hang up the phone.)

What thoughts come to mind when you read the above statement?

_____
_____
_____
_____
_____
_____
_____

Where are you today? Are you successful in this? Why or why not?

_____
_____
_____
_____
_____
_____
_____

Extreme Success: 90 DAY Devotional Journal

What is blocking your success in achieving this?

_____
_____
_____
_____
_____
_____
_____

Consider one or two steps of implementing your success:

_____
_____
_____
_____
_____
_____
_____

Find scriptures to support your success today:

_____
_____
_____
_____
_____
_____
_____

EXTREME THOUGHT: DAY 17

Leaders in Christ, remember this, "People only celebrate your failures when they fear your success".

(Write on a piece of paper, "SUCCESS".)

What thoughts come to mind when you read the above statement?

_____
_____
_____
_____
_____
_____
_____

Where are you today? Are you successful in this? Why or why not?

_____
_____
_____
_____
_____
_____
_____

Extreme Success: 90 DAY Devotional Journal

What is blocking your success in achieving this?

_____
_____
_____
_____
_____
_____
_____

Consider one or two steps of implementing your success:

_____
_____
_____
_____
_____
_____
_____

Find scriptures to support your success today:

_____
_____
_____
_____
_____
_____
_____

EXTREME THOUGHT: DAY 18

Stay in your place with Jesus. Don't be weary, stressed nor unfocused. When you're in position and ready to be launched, God will use His established plan for you, in you, and through you.

(Say out loud, "I'm staying in my place".)

What thoughts come to mind when you read the above statement?

_____
_____
_____
_____
_____
_____
_____

Where are you today? Are you successful in this? Why or why not?

_____
_____
_____
_____
_____
_____
_____

Extreme Success: 90 DAY Devotional Journal

What is blocking your success in achieving this?

_____
_____
_____
_____
_____
_____
_____

Consider one or two steps of implementing your success:

_____
_____
_____
_____
_____
_____
_____

Find scriptures to support your success today:

_____
_____
_____
_____
_____
_____
_____

EXTREME THOUGHT: DAY 19

Your faith is getting s, st, str, stro, stron, strong, stronge, stronger every moment in Jesus. Look back and you will see growth. It's evident & obvious. stronGER!!

(Shake your fist in the air and yell, "I am stronger".)

What thoughts come to mind when you read the above statement?

_____
_____
_____
_____
_____
_____
_____

Where are you today? Are you successful in this? Why or why not?

_____
_____
_____
_____
_____
_____
_____

Extreme Success: 90 DAY Devotional Journal

What is blocking your success in achieving this?

_____
_____
_____
_____
_____
_____
_____

Consider one or two steps of implementing your success:

_____
_____
_____
_____
_____
_____
_____

Find scriptures to support your success today:

_____
_____
_____
_____
_____
_____
_____

EXTREME THOUGHT: DAY 20

You've been set up by Jesus to receive your greatest blessing. He allowed you to suffer, fight and almost be defeated so that He could prove Himself to you that He is your God. It's all a set up!

(Call your pastor and tell them, "It's a set up".)

What thoughts come to mind when you read the above statement?

_____
_____
_____
_____
_____
_____
_____

Where are you today? Are you successful in this? Why or why not?

_____
_____
_____
_____
_____
_____
_____

Extreme Success: 90 DAY Devotional Journal

What is blocking your success in achieving this?

___

Consider one or two steps of implementing your success:

___

Find scriptures to support your success today:

___

EXTREME THOUGHT: DAY 21

Push, shove, bombard and trample your way into the secret place of God and then stay there. The enemy can't find you there. Press into His presence. Jesus is waiting to see you.

(Play the song, "Press in your presence by Shana Wilson" and get in His secret place with worship).

What thoughts come to mind when you read the above statement?

_____
_____
_____
_____
_____
_____
_____

Where are you today? Are you successful in this? Why or why not?

_____
_____
_____
_____
_____
_____

Extreme Success: 90 DAY Devotional Journal

What is blocking your success in achieving this?

Consider one or two steps of implementing your success:

Find scriptures to support your success today:

EXTREME THOUGHT: DAY 22

Just believe today Jesus heard your cry and He's moving heaven and earth to change your life. You haven't been forgotten, left out, nor a castaway. That mountain WILL BE MOVED!

(Text ten people and tell them, "Your mountain will be removed, God heard your cry".)

What thoughts come to mind when you read the above statement?

_____
_____
_____
_____
_____
_____
_____

Where are you today? Are you successful in this? Why or why not?

_____
_____
_____
_____
_____
_____
_____

Extreme Success: 90 DAY Devotional Journal

What is blocking your success in achieving this?

_____
_____
_____
_____
_____
_____
_____

Consider one or two steps of implementing your success:

_____
_____
_____
_____
_____
_____
_____

Find scriptures to support your success today:

_____
_____
_____
_____
_____
_____
_____

EXTREME THOUGHT: DAY 23

Christ has given you true, prevailing and everlasting freedom from the enemy's snares, traps, deceit and failures! You are free to be free and be who Jesus made you to be. No boundaries.

(Post this on your social media page, "No boundaries".)

What thoughts come to mind when you read the above statement?

_____
_____
_____
_____
_____
_____
_____

Where are you today? Are you successful in this? Why or why not?

_____
_____
_____
_____
_____
_____
_____

Extreme Success: 90 DAY Devotional Journal

What is blocking your success in achieving this?

_____
_____
_____
_____
_____
_____
_____

Consider one or two steps of implementing your success:

_____
_____
_____
_____
_____
_____
_____

Find scriptures to support your success today:

_____
_____
_____
_____
_____
_____
_____

EXTREME THOUGHT: DAY 24

They counted you out and said it's over! They claimed you would never be who Jesus called you to be. THEY WERE WRONG! Their mouths are now shut! Your best time is now!

(Say out loud, "They were wrong".)

What thoughts come to mind when you read the above statement?

_____
_____
_____
_____
_____
_____

Where are you today? Are you successful in this? Why or why not?

_____
_____
_____
_____
_____
_____
_____

Extreme Success: 90 DAY Devotional Journal

What is blocking your success in achieving this?

Consider one or two steps of implementing your success:

Find scriptures to support your success today:

EXTREME THOUGHT: DAY 25

There's been so much rain in your life that many times you don't believe the SON is still shining. Nevertheless, your rain is about to turn into SONSHINE. Look up, the clouds are parting, and your season is changing.

(Get out your umbrella. Go outside, open your umbrella, and say, "My rain is ending, the Son is coming out". Now close your umbrella; you won't need it anymore.)

What thoughts come to mind when you read the above statement?

_____
_____
_____
_____
_____
_____
_____

*Where are you today? Are you successful in this?
Why or why not?*

_____
_____
_____
_____
_____
_____
_____

Extreme Success: 90 DAY Devotional Journal

What is blocking your success in achieving this?

_____
_____
_____
_____
_____
_____
_____

Consider one or two steps of implementing your success:

_____
_____
_____
_____
_____
_____
_____

Find scriptures to support your success today:

_____
_____
_____
_____
_____
_____
_____

EXTREME THOUGHT: DAY 26

Be strong when you don't feel strong! Be brave if you don't feel brave! Rejoice even when you don't feel like rejoicing! Don't be led by your feelings, Be led by your faith.

(Tell everyone in your house this phrase today and give them a high five).

What thoughts come to mind when you read the above statement?

_____
_____
_____
_____
_____
_____
_____

Where are you today? Are you successful in this? Why or why not?

_____
_____
_____
_____
_____
_____
_____

Extreme Success: 90 DAY Devotional Journal

What is blocking your success in achieving this?

_____
_____
_____
_____
_____
_____
_____

Consider one or two steps of implementing your success:

_____
_____
_____
_____
_____
_____
_____

Find scriptures to support your success today:

_____
_____
_____
_____
_____
_____
_____

EXTREME THOUGHT: DAY 27

Your greatest victory is not when you win, but when you stumble, crash and fall. You must decide to get back up to fight! Allow your setbacks to transform you for your comeback.

(Post on social media today, "Get back up and fight".)

What thoughts come to mind when you read the above statement?

_____
_____
_____
_____
_____
_____
_____

Where are you today? Are you successful in this? Why or why not?

_____
_____
_____
_____
_____
_____
_____

Extreme Success: 90 DAY Devotional Journal

What is blocking your success in achieving this?

_____
_____
_____
_____
_____
_____
_____

Consider one or two steps of implementing your success:

_____
_____
_____
_____
_____
_____
_____

Find scriptures to support your success today:

_____
_____
_____
_____
_____
_____
_____

EXTREME THOUGHT: DAY 28

Jesus said to take your next step in faith because this step is going to change your entire life. Don't second guess, ponder or wonder. STEP when He says STEP! He's got you! Now step.

(Take steps in your home and say, "My faith is building".)

What thoughts come to mind when you read the above statement?

_____
_____
_____
_____
_____
_____
_____

Where are you today? Are you successful in this? Why or why not?

_____
_____
_____
_____
_____
_____
_____

Extreme Success: 90 DAY Devotional Journal

What is blocking your success in achieving this?

_____
_____
_____
_____
_____
_____
_____

Consider one or two steps of implementing your success:

_____
_____
_____
_____
_____
_____
_____

Find scriptures to support your success today:

_____
_____
_____
_____
_____
_____
_____

EXTREME THOUGHT: DAY 29

I am going to MAKE IT, OVERCOME IT, CONQUER IT, TRIUMPH OVER IT, DEFEAT IT & WIN IN IT!

(Repeat five times)

What thoughts come to mind when you read the above statement?

_____
_____
_____
_____
_____
_____

Where are you today? Are you successful in this? Why or why not?

_____
_____
_____
_____
_____
_____

Extreme Success: 90 DAY Devotional Journal

What is blocking your success in achieving this?

_____
_____
_____
_____
_____
_____
_____

Consider one or two steps of implementing your success:

_____
_____
_____
_____
_____
_____
_____

Find scriptures to support your success today:

_____
_____
_____
_____
_____
_____
_____

EXTREME THOUGHT: DAY 30

Just believe that when the enemy tries to stress you out, Jesus comes in to bless you out. Your blessed days are GREATER than your stressed days! MORE blessed than stressed!

(Write a note saying, "I am blessed and not stressed", and it place on your mirror.)

What thoughts come to mind when you read the above statement?

_____
_____
_____
_____
_____
_____
_____

Where are you today? Are you successful in this? Why or why not?

_____
_____
_____
_____
_____
_____
_____

Extreme Success: 90 DAY Devotional Journal

What is blocking your success in achieving this?

Consider one or two steps of implementing your success:

Find scriptures to support your success today:

EXTREME Success ☑

SECTION 2

DAYS 31 - 60

Becoming a bolder you!

Joshua 1:9 (TLB)

"Yes, be bold and strong! Banish fear and doubt! For remember, the Lord your God is with you wherever you go."

EXTREME THOUGHT: DAY 31

Your winter season has come to an end. In the Spirit, you can see buds emerging from the ground so don't give up. Be patient! Blessings are about to bloom. IT WILL AMAZE you!

(Buy yourself a flower today as a reminder of this.)

What thoughts come to mind when you read the above statement?

_____
_____
_____
_____
_____
_____

Where are you today? Are you successful in this? Why or why not?

_____
_____
_____
_____
_____
_____

Extreme Success: 90 DAY Devotional Journal

What is blocking your success in achieving this?

_____
_____
_____
_____
_____
_____
_____

Consider one or two steps of implementing your success:

_____
_____
_____
_____
_____
_____
_____

Find scriptures to support your success today:

_____
_____
_____
_____
_____
_____
_____

EXTREME THOUGHT: DAY 32

Don't let a setback prevent your comeback! Pick yourself up, wipe off the dirt, adjust your posture, and determine in your mind that you are moving forward in Jesus!

(Play the song, "Moving forward" by Hezekiah Walker.)

What thoughts come to mind when you read the above statement?

___

Where are you today? Are you successful in this? Why or why not?

___

Extreme Success: 90 DAY Devotional Journal

What is blocking your success in achieving this?

_____
_____
_____
_____
_____
_____
_____

Consider one or two steps of implementing your success:

_____
_____
_____
_____
_____
_____
_____

Find scriptures to support your success today:

_____
_____
_____
_____
_____
_____
_____

EXTREME THOUGHT: DAY 33

Your greatest victory comes after your greatest struggle. You can't give up your destiny! Fight with crazy faith and you'll have crazy victory! YOUR ONLY ONE STEP AWAY! TAKE YOUR STEP!

(Continue taking steps in your home like you did last week.)

What thoughts come to mind when you read the above statement?

_____
_____
_____
_____
_____
_____
_____

Where are you today? Are you successful in this? Why or why not?

_____
_____
_____
_____
_____
_____
_____

Extreme Success: 90 DAY Devotional Journal

What is blocking your success in achieving this?

_____
_____
_____
_____
_____
_____
_____

Consider one or two steps of implementing your success:

_____
_____
_____
_____
_____
_____
_____

Find scriptures to support your success today:

_____
_____
_____
_____
_____
_____
_____

EXTREME THOUGHT: DAY 34

Ask God today for what you need! He wants to give you the desires of your heart and bless you. Speak out loud, "He will bless me EXCEEDING ABUNDANTLY ABOVE what I can ask or think"! He just inclined His ear to hear you. ASK!

What thoughts come to mind when you read the above statement?

_____
_____
_____
_____
_____
_____
_____

*Where are you today? Are you successful in this?
Why or why not?*

_____
_____
_____
_____
_____
_____
_____

Extreme Success: 90 DAY Devotional Journal

What is blocking your success in achieving this?

_____
_____
_____
_____
_____
_____
_____

Consider one or two steps of implementing your success:

_____
_____
_____
_____
_____
_____
_____

Find scriptures to support your success today:

_____
_____
_____
_____
_____
_____
_____

EXTREME THOUGHT: DAY 35

Your winter season is coming to an end. It's been tough, lonely, a major fight– attack after attack, stressful and draining. You made it through as Jesus promised. Dust the snow off your feet and move into spring.

(Text ten people and tell them, "Your season is changing for your good".)

What thoughts come to mind when you read the above statement?

_____
_____
_____
_____
_____
_____
_____
_____

Where are you today? Are you successful in this? Why or why not?

_____
_____
_____
_____
_____
_____
_____

Extreme Success: 90 DAY Devotional Journal

What is blocking your success in achieving this?

_____
_____
_____
_____
_____
_____
_____

Consider one or two steps of implementing your success:

_____
_____
_____
_____
_____
_____
_____

Find scriptures to support your success today:

_____
_____
_____
_____
_____
_____
_____

EXTREME THOUGHT: DAY 36

God is wonderful, majestic, awesome, powerful, mighty, sustaining, protective, healing, strong, destiny-driving, enemy-blocking, and enemy-stopping, WOW!

(Post this entire phrase on your social media.)

What thoughts come to mind when you read the above statement?

_____
_____
_____
_____
_____
_____

Where are you today? Are you successful in this? Why or why not?

_____
_____
_____
_____
_____
_____

Extreme Success: 90 DAY Devotional Journal

What is blocking your success in achieving this?

_____
_____
_____
_____
_____
_____

Consider one or two steps of implementing your success:

_____
_____
_____
_____
_____
_____

Find scriptures to support your success today:

_____
_____
_____
_____
_____
_____

EXTREME THOUGHT: DAY 37

Be determined that nothing will be able to distract, detour, nor stop you from your destiny in Christ! NO situation, NO trial, NO person, NO heartache, NOTHING!

(Say out loud, "NOTHING Devil"!)

What thoughts come to mind when you read the above statement?

_____
_____
_____
_____
_____
_____
_____

Where are you today? Are you successful in this? Why or why not?

_____
_____
_____
_____
_____
_____
_____

Extreme Success: 90 DAY Devotional Journal

What is blocking your success in achieving this?

_____
_____
_____
_____
_____
_____
_____

Consider one or two steps of implementing your success:

_____
_____
_____
_____
_____
_____
_____

Find scriptures to support your success today:

_____
_____
_____
_____
_____
_____
_____

EXTREME THOUGHT: DAY 38

God's faithfulness is automatic for His people. He doesn't have to think about it, ponder on it or consider it, it is automatic. It's who He is. It's for you, Faithful!

(Write on a note and place on your mirror, "God's faithfulness is automatic".)

What thoughts come to mind when you read the above statement?

_____
_____
_____
_____
_____
_____
_____

Where are you today? Are you successful in this? Why or why not?

_____
_____
_____
_____
_____
_____
_____
_____

Extreme Success: 90 DAY Devotional Journal

What is blocking your success in achieving this?

_____
_____
_____
_____
_____
_____
_____

Consider one or two steps of implementing your success:

_____
_____
_____
_____
_____
_____
_____

Find scriptures to support your success today:

_____
_____
_____
_____
_____
_____
_____

EXTREME THOUGHT: DAY 39

Say, "I will overcome! I will triumph! I will conquer! I will succeed! I will persist! I will defeat! I will not back down! I must prevail in Jesus!"

(Email this quote to five people.)

What thoughts come to mind when you read the above statement?

_____
_____
_____
_____
_____
_____

Where are you today? Are you successful in this? Why or why not?

_____
_____
_____
_____
_____
_____

Extreme Success: 90 DAY Devotional Journal

What is blocking your success in achieving this?

_____
_____
_____
_____
_____
_____
_____

Consider one or two steps of implementing your success:

_____
_____
_____
_____
_____
_____
_____

Find scriptures to support your success today:

_____
_____
_____
_____
_____
_____
_____

EXTREME THOUGHT: DAY 40

Tell the devil, "I'm still here!" You didn't kill me, steal from me nor destroy me!! The tactics failed, the plan fell apart and you didn't succeed. I'M STILL HERE!

(On a note write "I'm still here", and put it on your mirror.)

What thoughts come to mind when you read the above statement?

_____
_____
_____
_____
_____
_____
_____

Where are you today? Are you successful in this? Why or why not?

_____
_____
_____
_____
_____
_____
_____

Extreme Success: 90 DAY Devotional Journal

What is blocking your success in achieving this?

_____
_____
_____
_____
_____
_____
_____

Consider one or two steps of implementing your success:

_____
_____
_____
_____
_____
_____
_____

Find scriptures to support your success today:

_____
_____
_____
_____
_____
_____
_____

EXTREME THOUGHT: DAY 41

Warning! We have a sneaky devil alert from the National Jesus Authority! Be prepared and wise of the enemy's tactics! If you set your mind to win, you will not be affected! This is only a test.

(Say out loud, "This is only a test".)

What thoughts come to mind when you read the above statement?

_____
_____
_____
_____
_____
_____
_____

Where are you today? Are you successful in this? Why or why not?

_____
_____
_____
_____
_____
_____
_____

Extreme Success: 90 DAY Devotional Journal

What is blocking your success in achieving this?

_____
_____
_____
_____
_____
_____
_____

Consider one or two steps of implementing your success:

_____
_____
_____
_____
_____
_____
_____

Find scriptures to support your success today:

_____
_____
_____
_____
_____
_____
_____

EXTREME THOUGHT: DAY 42

God is making a transformation! You may not see it or feel it yet, but it's there! God is doing things behind the scene. Just wait. It's coming; you will be amazed!

(Post on social media, "Just wait, it's coming from God".)

What thoughts come to mind when you read the above statement?

_____
_____
_____
_____
_____
_____

Where are you today? Are you successful in this? Why or why not?

_____
_____
_____
_____
_____
_____

Extreme Success: 90 DAY Devotional Journal

What is blocking your success in achieving this?

_____
_____
_____
_____
_____
_____
_____

Consider one or two steps of implementing your success:

_____
_____
_____
_____
_____
_____
_____

Find scriptures to support your success today:

_____
_____
_____
_____
_____
_____
_____

EXTREME THOUGHT: DAY 43

Your greatest victories have yet to be seen. You have won some battles, lost many battles, and have been devastated by a few. God has kept you through them all. You will see your GREATER soon!

(Write on a note and place on your mirror, "My greater is here".)

What thoughts come to mind when you read the above statement?

Where are you today? Are you successful in this? Why or why not?

Extreme Success: 90 DAY Devotional Journal

What is blocking your success in achieving this?

_____
_____
_____
_____
_____
_____
_____

Consider one or two steps of implementing your success:

_____
_____
_____
_____
_____
_____
_____

Find scriptures to support your success today:

_____
_____
_____
_____
_____
_____
_____

EXTREME THOUGHT: DAY 44

You are FREE in the Lord. FREE to dance, FREE to sing, FREE to hear, FREE to worship, FREE to praise, FREE from distractions, FREE from haters, FREE to live in Jesus!

(Call a family member today that you haven't seen for a while to encourage them with this thought.)

What thoughts come to mind when you read the above statement?

_____
_____
_____
_____
_____
_____
_____

Where are you today? Are you successful in this? Why or why not?

_____
_____
_____
_____
_____
_____
_____

Extreme Success: 90 DAY Devotional Journal

What is blocking your success in achieving this?

_____
_____
_____
_____
_____
_____
_____

Consider one or two steps of implementing your success:

_____
_____
_____
_____
_____
_____
_____

Find scriptures to support your success today:

_____
_____
_____
_____
_____
_____
_____

EXTREME THOUGHT: DAY 45

Don't allow your mind to speak the opposite of what God said to you! Your mind is not in control, God is! Tell your mind to "shut up" because God is speaking.

(Say out loud, "Shut up mind".)

What thoughts come to mind when you read the above statement?

_____
_____
_____
_____
_____
_____

Where are you today? Are you successful in this? Why or why not?

_____
_____
_____
_____
_____
_____

Extreme Success: 90 DAY Devotional Journal

What is blocking your success in achieving this?

_____
_____
_____
_____
_____
_____
_____

Consider one or two steps of implementing your success:

_____
_____
_____
_____
_____
_____
_____

Find scriptures to support your success today:

_____
_____
_____
_____
_____
_____
_____

EXTREME THOUGHT: DAY 46

Jesus loves you so much! Jesus loves you so much! Jesus loves you so much! Jesus loves you so much! Jesus loves you so much! Jesus loves you so much!
DON'T FORGET THIS!

(Post this on social media today.)

What thoughts come to mind when you read the above statement?

_____
_____
_____
_____
_____
_____

Where are you today? Are you successful in this? Why or why not?

_____
_____
_____
_____
_____

What is blocking your success in achieving this?

_____
_____
_____
_____
_____
_____
_____

Consider one or two steps of implementing your success:

_____
_____
_____
_____
_____
_____
_____

Find scriptures to support your success today:

_____
_____
_____
_____
_____
_____
_____

EXTREME THOUGHT: DAY 47

You are so important to Jesus that He said, "I WILL NOT leave you, forsake you, or relax My hold on you. I have you secured tightly. You are mine.

(Write on a note and place on your mirror, "I am His".)

What thoughts come to mind when you read the above statement?

_____
_____
_____
_____
_____
_____
_____

Where are you today? Are you successful in this? Why or why not?

_____
_____
_____
_____
_____
_____
_____

Extreme Success: 90 DAY Devotional Journal

What is blocking your success in achieving this?

_____
_____
_____
_____
_____
_____
_____

Consider one or two steps of implementing your success:

_____
_____
_____
_____
_____
_____
_____

Find scriptures to support your success today:

_____
_____
_____
_____
_____
_____
_____

EXTREME THOUGHT: DAY 48

Let the fake people go! Don't hold on to people that you love that don't love you! Who said they had to be in your life to complete you? You only need Jesus to complete you.

(The next person you see, tell them, "You only need Jesus to complete you".)

What thoughts come to mind when you read the above statement?

_____
_____
_____
_____
_____
_____
_____

Where are you today? Are you successful in this? Why or why not?

_____
_____
_____
_____
_____
_____
_____

Extreme Success: 90 DAY Devotional Journal

What is blocking your success in achieving this?

_____
_____
_____
_____
_____
_____
_____

Consider one or two steps of implementing your success:

_____
_____
_____
_____
_____
_____
_____

Find scriptures to support your success today:

_____
_____
_____
_____
_____
_____
_____

EXTREME THOUGHT: DAY 49

God said to get a napkin and speak your problem into it. Throw it on the floor and stomp it. Then say, "I am done with this problem". Pick up the napkin and throw it in the trash. It's over!

(Get your napkin and speak!)

What thoughts come to mind when you read the above statement?

_____
_____
_____
_____
_____
_____
_____

Where are you today? Are you successful in this? Why or why not?

_____
_____
_____
_____
_____
_____
_____

Extreme Success: 90 DAY Devotional Journal

What is blocking your success in achieving this?

_____
_____
_____
_____
_____
_____
_____

Consider one or two steps of implementing your success:

_____
_____
_____
_____
_____
_____
_____

Find scriptures to support your success today:

_____
_____
_____
_____
_____
_____
_____

EXTREME THOUGHT: DAY 50

HEALING! Today, I believe Jesus is healing you! He is making you whole. He is healing you for your FUTURE ASSIGNMENT!

(Touch the place on your body that is hurting. Begin to pray and then say, "I am healed".)

What thoughts come to mind when you read the above statement?

_____
_____
_____
_____
_____
_____

Where are you today? Are you successful in this? Why or why not?

_____
_____
_____
_____
_____
_____
_____

Extreme Success: 90 DAY Devotional Journal

What is blocking your success in achieving this?

_____
_____
_____
_____
_____
_____

Consider one or two steps of implementing your success:

_____
_____
_____
_____
_____
_____

Find scriptures to support your success today:

_____
_____
_____
_____
_____
_____

EXTREME THOUGHT: DAY 51

Stop battling the battle. Battle against the enemy! When you fight your battle, you have more stress and anxiety. When you fight the devil, you have more victory and endurance because God has given you authority over him in Jesus name. So, take your hands off of the battle. Put your faith in the victory!

(Write on a note and place it on your mirror, "I took my hands off the battle".)

What thoughts come to mind when you read the above statement?

_____
_____
_____
_____
_____
_____
_____

Where are you today? Are you successful in this? Why or why not?

_____
_____
_____
_____
_____
_____

Extreme Success: 90 DAY Devotional Journal

What is blocking your success in achieving this?

_____
_____
_____
_____
_____
_____
_____

Consider one or two steps of implementing your success:

_____
_____
_____
_____
_____
_____
_____

Find scriptures to support your success today:

_____
_____
_____
_____
_____
_____
_____

EXTREME THOUGHT: DAY 52

Jesus created you to listen and respond to His voice only! The more you know Him, the more you recognize when He's speaking. He is ready to give you an answer. LISTEN!

(Ask God to speak to your heart. Don't say anything else. Wait for Him to respond.)

What thoughts come to mind when you read the above statement?

_____
_____
_____
_____
_____
_____

Where are you today? Are you successful in this? Why or why not?

_____
_____
_____
_____
_____
_____

Extreme Success: 90 DAY Devotional Journal

What is blocking your success in achieving this?

_____
_____
_____
_____
_____
_____
_____

Consider one or two steps of implementing your success:

_____
_____
_____
_____
_____
_____
_____

Find scriptures to support your success today:

_____
_____
_____
_____
_____
_____
_____

EXTREME THOUGHT: DAY 53

Don't get upset when Jesus gives you an answer that you did not expect! You prayed for His will. He knows what's best for you! Trust His decision.

(Text six people and tell them, "Trust God's decision in your life".)

What thoughts come to mind when you read the above statement?

_____
_____
_____
_____
_____
_____

Where are you today? Are you successful in this? Why or why not?

_____
_____
_____
_____
_____
_____

Extreme Success: 90 DAY Devotional Journal

What is blocking your success in achieving this?

_____
_____
_____
_____
_____
_____

Consider one or two steps of implementing your success:

_____
_____
_____
_____
_____
_____

Find scriptures to support your success today:

_____
_____
_____
_____
_____
_____

EXTREME THOUGHT: DAY 54

Remember, you must win this battle. You are so close to your victory. Giving up is not an option. Stand a little while longer. You must win this battle.

(Write on a note and place it on your mirror, "Giving up is not an option".)

What thoughts come to mind when you read the above statement?

___

Where are you today? Are you successful in this? Why or why not?

___

Extreme Success: 90 DAY Devotional Journal

What is blocking your success in achieving this?

_____
_____
_____
_____
_____
_____
_____

Consider one or two steps of implementing your success:

_____
_____
_____
_____
_____
_____
_____

Find scriptures to support your success today:

_____
_____
_____
_____
_____
_____
_____

EXTREME THOUGHT: DAY 55

Speak out loud, "the devil is defeated"! (Louder) The devil is defeated! (Louder) The devil is defeated! (Repeat until you believe it) THE devil IS DEFEATED!

What thoughts come to mind when you read the above statement?

_____
_____
_____
_____
_____
_____
_____

Where are you today? Are you successful in this? Why or why not?

_____
_____
_____
_____
_____
_____
_____

Extreme Success: 90 DAY Devotional Journal

What is blocking your success in achieving this?

_____
_____
_____
_____
_____
_____
_____

Consider one or two steps of implementing your success:

_____
_____
_____
_____
_____
_____
_____

Find scriptures to support your success today:

_____
_____
_____
_____
_____
_____
_____

EXTREME THOUGHT: DAY 56

Just as the car mirror says, "objects are closer than what they appear", God says "your victory is closer than it appears"! Continue see it as God does!

(If you have a car, sit in the driver's seat. Look in the mirror and say, "my victory is closer than it appears".) Say it again and believe it. (If you do not have access to a vehicle, speak the phrase out loud wherever you are.)

What thoughts come to mind when you read the above statement?

_____
_____
_____
_____
_____
_____
_____

Where are you today? Are you successful in this? Why or why not?

_____
_____
_____
_____
_____
_____
_____

Extreme Success: 90 DAY Devotional Journal

What is blocking your success in achieving this?

_____
_____
_____
_____
_____
_____
_____

Consider one or two steps of implementing your success:

_____
_____
_____
_____
_____
_____
_____

Find scriptures to support your success today:

_____
_____
_____
_____
_____
_____
_____

EXTREME THOUGHT: DAY 57

Do you have heart problems - unforgiveness, bitterness, depression, anger, and malice? Well, Jesus is the cure. Accept His peace, joy and love today!

(Tell yourself, "I will forgive those who have devastated me". Then, call out everyone's name that you need to forgive and say, "I love _".)

What thoughts come to mind when you read the above statement?

_____
_____
_____
_____
_____
_____
_____

Where are you today? Are you successful in this? Why or why not?

_____
_____
_____
_____
_____
_____

Extreme Success: 90 DAY Devotional Journal

What is blocking your success in achieving this?

_____
_____
_____
_____
_____
_____
_____

Consider one or two steps of implementing your success:

_____
_____
_____
_____
_____
_____
_____

Find scriptures to support your success today:

_____
_____
_____
_____
_____
_____
_____

EXTREME THOUGHT: DAY 58

Remember, you are BLESSED, so you won't be STRESSED! Write down all God has done for you and show the enemy the list of your BLESSINGS when stress tries to come!

(Write down key blessings over the past few years and place it on your refrigerator as a reminder of what God has done.)

What thoughts come to mind when you read the above statement?

_____
_____
_____
_____
_____
_____
_____

Where are you today? Are you successful in this? Why or why not?

_____
_____
_____
_____
_____
_____
_____

Extreme Success: 90 DAY Devotional Journal

What is blocking your success in achieving this?

_____
_____
_____
_____
_____
_____
_____

Consider one or two steps of implementing your success:

_____
_____
_____
_____
_____
_____
_____

Find scriptures to support your success today:

_____
_____
_____
_____
_____
_____
_____

EXTREME THOUGHT: DAY 59

Don't look at who you are today to determine who God says you are tomorrow. God says you are blessed, rich, healthy, anointed, wise and an overcomer!

(Email your friends and send them this quote.)

What thoughts come to mind when you read the above statement?

_____
_____
_____
_____
_____
_____
_____

Where are you today? Are you successful in this? Why or why not?

_____
_____
_____
_____
_____
_____
_____

Extreme Success: 90 DAY Devotional Journal

What is blocking your success in achieving this?

_____
_____
_____
_____
_____
_____
_____

Consider one or two steps of implementing your success:

_____
_____
_____
_____
_____
_____
_____

Find scriptures to support your success today:

_____
_____
_____
_____
_____
_____
_____

EXTREME THOUGHT: DAY 60

You can't allow people's opinions, attitudes, inconsistencies or flakiness to stop what Jesus is doing in you. If they can't support you, "shake the dust off your feet" and move on.

(Say out loud, "I've moved on".)

What thoughts come to mind when you read the above statement?

Where are you today? Are you successful in this? Why or why not?

Extreme Success: 90 DAY Devotional Journal

What is blocking your success in achieving this?

_____
_____
_____
_____
_____
_____
_____

Consider one or two steps of implementing your success:

_____
_____
_____
_____
_____
_____
_____

Find scriptures to support your success today:

_____
_____
_____
_____
_____
_____
_____

EXTREME Success ☑

SECTION 3

DAYS 61 - 90

Make the decision: Prepare for the MOVE!

Isaiah 43:19

"Behold, I will do a new thing; now it shall spring forth; shall ye not know it?"

EXTREME THOUGHT: DAY 61

You are blessed more than you think! You are blessed more than you think! You are blessed more than you think! You are just blessed more!!!

(Post this statement on your social media.)

What thoughts come to mind when you read the above statement?

_____
_____
_____
_____
_____
_____
_____

Where are you today? Are you successful in this? Why or why not?

_____
_____
_____
_____
_____
_____
_____

Extreme Success: 90 DAY Devotional Journal

What is blocking your success in achieving this?

_____
_____
_____
_____
_____
_____
_____

Consider one or two steps of implementing your success:

_____
_____
_____
_____
_____
_____
_____

Find scriptures to support your success today:

_____
_____
_____
_____
_____
_____
_____

EXTREME THOUGHT: DAY 62

Jesus is making you into a bolder you! Aggressive to fight, win, and overcome every time. You can not back down to the enemy!

(Play the song on YouTube, "I Win" by Clint Brown.)

What thoughts come to mind when you read the above statement?

_____
_____
_____
_____
_____
_____
_____

Where are you today? Are you successful in this? Why or why not?

_____
_____
_____
_____
_____
_____
_____

Extreme Success: 90 DAY Devotional Journal

What is blocking your success in achieving this?

_____
_____
_____
_____
_____
_____
_____

Consider one or two steps of implementing your success:

_____
_____
_____
_____
_____
_____
_____

Find scriptures to support your success today:

_____
_____
_____
_____
_____
_____
_____

EXTREME THOUGHT: DAY 63

Believe today no matter what. Believe today no matter who doesn't! Believe today no matter how bad the situation is. Believe today!!!!

(Make up your own song and sing, "I believe today".)

What thoughts come to mind when you read the above statement?

_____
_____
_____
_____
_____
_____
_____

Where are you today? Are you successful in this? Why or why not?

_____
_____
_____
_____
_____
_____
_____

Extreme Success: 90 DAY Devotional Journal

What is blocking your success in achieving this?

_____
_____
_____
_____
_____
_____

Consider one or two steps of implementing your success:

_____
_____
_____
_____
_____
_____

Find scriptures to support your success today:

_____
_____
_____
_____
_____
_____

EXTREME THOUGHT: DAY 64

YOU MUST ENTER TO WIN! You've got to enter God's presence and stay there for you to win the fight that you are in. God has already drawn your name and you have won!

(Post on social media, "You must enter to win".)

What thoughts come to mind when you read the above statement?

_____
_____
_____
_____
_____
_____
_____

Where are you today? Are you successful in this? Why or why not?

_____
_____
_____
_____
_____
_____
_____

Extreme Success: 90 DAY Devotional Journal

What is blocking your success in achieving this?

Consider one or two steps of implementing your success:

Find scriptures to support your success today:

EXTREME THOUGHT: DAY 65

DELIVERANCE! The temptation you've been struggling with, God has given you strength to once and for all overcome it. You've finally won!

(Play the song on YouTube "Shake the foundation" by Clint Brown.)

What thoughts come to mind when you read the above statement?

_____
_____
_____
_____
_____
_____

Where are you today? Are you successful in this? Why or why not?

_____
_____
_____
_____
_____
_____

Extreme Success: 90 DAY Devotional Journal

What is blocking your success in achieving this?

_____
_____
_____
_____
_____
_____
_____

Consider one or two steps of implementing your success:

_____
_____
_____
_____
_____
_____

Find scriptures to support your success today:

_____
_____
_____
_____
_____
_____

EXTREME THOUGHT: DAY 66

Repeat to yourself, " I have won, I have conquered, I have victory, I have faith, I have joy, I have favor, I have strength, I have boldness, I have Jesus!

(Repeat out loud five times.)

What thoughts come to mind when you read the above statement?

_____
_____
_____
_____
_____
_____

Where are you today? Are you successful in this? Why or why not?

_____
_____
_____
_____
_____
_____

Extreme Success: 90 DAY Devotional Journal

What is blocking your success in achieving this?

_____
_____
_____
_____
_____
_____

Consider one or two steps of implementing your success:

_____
_____
_____
_____
_____
_____

Find scriptures to support your success today:

_____
_____
_____
_____
_____
_____

EXTREME THOUGHT: DAY 67

DO NOT doubt God! No matter the situation! You did hear the voice of God and you are on pace to accomplish your purpose.

(Tell your enemy, "blah, blah, blah! You are just making noise. I can't hear you"!)

What thoughts come to mind when you read the above statement?

_____
_____
_____
_____
_____
_____
_____

Where are you today? Are you successful in this? Why or why not?

_____
_____
_____
_____
_____
_____
_____

Extreme Success: 90 DAY Devotional Journal

What is blocking your success in achieving this?

_____
_____
_____
_____
_____
_____
_____

Consider one or two steps of implementing your success:

_____
_____
_____
_____
_____
_____
_____

Find scriptures to support your success today:

_____
_____
_____
_____
_____
_____
_____

EXTREME THOUGHT: DAY 68

Strength is when you feel your weakest, look the weakest, think the weakest and people say you are at your weakest! That's when God's strength takes over and you become SUPERMAN or WONDER WOMAN!

(Watch a Superhero movie. God is going to show you revelation. Have a notepad and pen to write what God shows you.)

What thoughts come to mind when you read the above statement?

_____
_____
_____
_____
_____
_____
_____

Where are you today? Are you successful in this? Why or why not?

_____
_____
_____
_____
_____
_____

Extreme Success: 90 DAY Devotional Journal

What is blocking your success in achieving this?

_____
_____
_____
_____
_____
_____

Consider one or two steps of implementing your success:

_____
_____
_____
_____
_____
_____

Find scriptures to support your success today:

_____
_____
_____
_____
_____
_____

EXTREME THOUGHT: DAY 69

You don't have to prove yourself to anyone. Focus on proving yourself faithful to Jesus. He's the only one that can position your eternity. Prove and continue to improve!

(Say out loud, "I am better now from when I started this 90 day journal. I have improved".)

What thoughts come to mind when you read the above statement?

_____
_____
_____
_____
_____
_____
_____

Where are you today? Are you successful in this? Why or why not?

_____
_____
_____
_____
_____
_____

Extreme Success: 90 DAY Devotional Journal

What is blocking your success in achieving this?

_____
_____
_____
_____
_____
_____
_____

Consider one or two steps of implementing your success:

_____
_____
_____
_____
_____
_____
_____

Find scriptures to support your success today:

_____
_____
_____
_____
_____
_____
_____

EXTREME THOUGHT: DAY 70

God is asking today, "DO YOU TRUST ME"? That's all that God asks today!

(Write on a note, "Just trust God" and place on your mirror.)

What thoughts come to mind when you read the above statement?

_____
_____
_____
_____
_____
_____
_____

Where are you today? Are you successful in this? Why or why not?

_____
_____
_____
_____
_____
_____
_____

Extreme Success: 90 DAY Devotional Journal

What is blocking your success in achieving this?

_____
_____
_____
_____
_____
_____
_____

Consider one or two steps of implementing your success:

_____
_____
_____
_____
_____
_____
_____

Find scriptures to support your success today:

_____
_____
_____
_____
_____
_____
_____

EXTREME THOUGHT: DAY 71

Listen! Do you hear the voice of the Lord? He speaks to you in a still, small voice! Stop what you're doing right now and listen! He's ready to speak! Listen! What's He saying?

(Write down what He is speaking to you.)

What thoughts come to mind when you read the above statement?

_____
_____
_____
_____
_____
_____
_____

Where are you today? Are you successful in this? Why or why not?

_____
_____
_____
_____
_____
_____
_____

Extreme Success: 90 DAY Devotional Journal

What is blocking your success in achieving this?

_____
_____
_____
_____
_____
_____
_____

Consider one or two steps of implementing your success:

_____
_____
_____
_____
_____
_____
_____

Find scriptures to support your success today:

_____
_____
_____
_____
_____
_____
_____

EXTREME THOUGHT: DAY 72

Count it done when Jesus takes control of your situation. If you don't take control back, it's done!

(In your issues, trials, setbacks and problems say, "I won't take it back. It is done"!)

What thoughts come to mind when you read the above statement?

_____
_____
_____
_____
_____
_____
_____

Where are you today? Are you successful in this? Why or why not?

_____
_____
_____
_____
_____
_____
_____

Extreme Success: 90 DAY Devotional Journal

What is blocking your success in achieving this?

_____
_____
_____
_____
_____
_____
_____

Consider one or two steps of implementing your success:

_____
_____
_____
_____
_____
_____
_____

Find scriptures to support your success today:

_____
_____
_____
_____
_____
_____
_____

EXTREME THOUGHT: DAY 73

Don't block God when you are in the fight. Block the enemy. God is not fighting against you, but for you. The enemy is NOT for you but against you. Fight for your life and continue to win every time!

(Play the song, "Put a praise on it" by Tasha Cobbs.)

What thoughts come to mind when you read the above statement?

_____
_____
_____
_____
_____
_____
_____

Where are you today? Are you successful in this? Why or why not?

_____
_____
_____
_____
_____
_____

Extreme Success: 90 DAY Devotional Journal

What is blocking your success in achieving this?

Consider one or two steps of implementing your success:

Find scriptures to support your success today:

EXTREME THOUGHT: DAY 74

Be excited, energetic, enthusiastic, joyous, happy, grateful, thankful in who God made you to be! There is nothing wrong with you! God made the best you He could. Be you in Jesus!

(Post this on your social media.)

What thoughts come to mind when you read the above statement?

_____
_____
_____
_____
_____
_____

Where are you today? Are you successful in this? Why or why not?

_____
_____
_____
_____
_____
_____

Extreme Success: 90 DAY Devotional Journal

What is blocking your success in achieving this?

_____
_____
_____
_____
_____
_____
_____

Consider one or two steps of implementing your success:

_____
_____
_____
_____
_____
_____
_____

Find scriptures to support your success today:

_____
_____
_____
_____
_____
_____
_____

EXTREME THOUGHT: DAY 75

Believe it! Receive it! Adopt it! Transform it! Live it! Walk it! Run to it! Rejoice in it! Proclaim it! Be bold in it! Don't fight it! "It" is God's promise to you!

(Call two friends today and tell them this statement to encourage them.)

What thoughts come to mind when you read the above statement?

___

Where are you today? Are you successful in this? Why or why not?

___

Extreme Success: 90 DAY Devotional Journal

What is blocking your success in achieving this?

_____
_____
_____
_____
_____
_____
_____

Consider one or two steps of implementing your success:

_____
_____
_____
_____
_____
_____
_____

Find scriptures to support your success today:

_____
_____
_____
_____
_____
_____
_____

EXTREME THOUGHT: DAY 76

Don't believe anything that the enemy still says about you. It's a conspiracy! It's a fraud and a lie! In this plot against you, listen only to Jesus. He speaks for you!

(Write on a note "It's a conspiracy" and place it on your mirror.)

What thoughts come to mind when you read the above statement?

Where are you today? Are you successful in this? Why or why not?

Extreme Success: 90 DAY Devotional Journal

What is blocking your success in achieving this?

_____
_____
_____
_____
_____
_____

Consider one or two steps of implementing your success:

_____
_____
_____
_____
_____
_____

Find scriptures to support your success today:

_____
_____
_____
_____
_____
_____

EXTREME THOUGHT: DAY 77

Just believe God! Just believe God! Just believe God! Just believe God! Just believe God! Just believe God! Just believe God! Just believe God! Just believe!

(Text twenty-eight people and tell them, "Just believe God!")

What thoughts come to mind when you read the above statement?

_____
_____
_____
_____
_____
_____
_____

Where are you today? Are you successful in this? Why or why not?

_____
_____
_____
_____
_____
_____
_____

Extreme Success: 90 DAY Devotional Journal

What is blocking your success in achieving this?

_____
_____
_____
_____
_____
_____
_____

Consider one or two steps of implementing your success:

_____
_____
_____
_____
_____
_____
_____

Find scriptures to support your success today:

_____
_____
_____
_____
_____
_____
_____

EXTREME THOUGHT: DAY 78

Determine to remain consistent in your faith regardless of external conditions. Discipline yourself not to waiver because of people. Say to yourself, "they won't sway me"!

(Sing the old song, "I shall not be moved".)

What thoughts come to mind when you read the above statement?

_____
_____
_____
_____
_____
_____
_____

Where are you today? Are you successful in this? Why or why not?

_____
_____
_____
_____
_____
_____
_____

Extreme Success: 90 DAY Devotional Journal

What is blocking your success in achieving this?

_____
_____
_____
_____
_____
_____

Consider one or two steps of implementing your success:

_____
_____
_____
_____
_____
_____

Find scriptures to support your success today:

_____
_____
_____
_____
_____
_____

EXTREME THOUGHT: DAY 79

Being a warrior with success and victory begins in your mind. Do you think and believe like an overcomer? Make sure your thoughts align with triumph & success. Think, fight, and win!

(Share this with your family today in your home and talk about what it means.)

What thoughts come to mind when you read the above statement?

_____
_____
_____
_____
_____
_____

Where are you today? Are you successful in this? Why or why not?

_____
_____
_____
_____
_____
_____

Extreme Success: 90 DAY Devotional Journal

What is blocking your success in achieving this?

_____
_____
_____
_____
_____
_____

Consider one or two steps of implementing your success:

_____
_____
_____
_____
_____
_____

Find scriptures to support your success today:

_____
_____
_____
_____
_____
_____

EXTREME THOUGHT: DAY 80

Block the punch the enemy throws! Now dunk down, stand up, and knock out the enemy! God has given you specific instructions to defeat the enemy every time! Act on it!

(Write on a note, "act on it" and place it on your mirror.)

What thoughts come to mind when you read the above statement?

_____
_____
_____
_____
_____
_____
_____

Where are you today? Are you successful in this? Why or why not?

_____
_____
_____
_____
_____
_____

Extreme Success: 90 DAY Devotional Journal

What is blocking your success in achieving this?

_____
_____
_____
_____
_____
_____

Consider one or two steps of implementing your success:

_____
_____
_____
_____
_____
_____

Find scriptures to support your success today:

_____
_____
_____
_____
_____
_____

EXTREME THOUGHT: DAY 81

God said you're "brave, bold, powerful, mighty, free, fierce, courageous, chosen, alive, extreme, rooted, contagious, overflowing, dominant, extravagant and His own!

(Post this on your social media, text a bunch of people, call two friends and email one person to encourage them all with this thought.)

What thoughts come to mind when you read the above statement?

_____
_____
_____
_____
_____
_____
_____

Where are you today? Are you successful in this? Why or why not?

_____
_____
_____
_____
_____
_____

Extreme Success: 90 DAY Devotional Journal

What is blocking your success in achieving this?

_____
_____
_____
_____
_____
_____
_____

Consider one or two steps of implementing your success:

_____
_____
_____
_____
_____
_____
_____

Find scriptures to support your success today:

_____
_____
_____
_____
_____
_____
_____

EXTREME THOUGHT: DAY 82

Joy in Jesus isn't based on how you feel, but by how you heal. I pray today the joy within you will rise, dominate, and motivate your inner man. Be consumed in Jesus' name.

(Pray today that as God has healed you from past hurts that those emotions will never rise again.)

What thoughts come to mind when you read the above statement?

_____
_____
_____
_____
_____
_____
_____

Where are you today? Are you successful in this? Why or why not?

_____
_____
_____
_____
_____
_____

Extreme Success: 90 DAY Devotional Journal

What is blocking your success in achieving this?

_____
_____
_____
_____
_____
_____
_____

Consider one or two steps of implementing your success:

_____
_____
_____
_____
_____
_____
_____

Find scriptures to support your success today:

_____
_____
_____
_____
_____
_____
_____

EXTREME THOUGHT: DAY 83

Rise! Pick up your sword! Put on your armor! Place on your helmet! Put on your breastplate! Put on your boots! Put on your belt! Tell the enemy, "enough is enough!" Fight!

(Say out loud, "enough is enough".)

What thoughts come to mind when you read the above statement?

_____
_____
_____
_____
_____
_____
_____

Where are you today? Are you successful in this? Why or why not?

_____
_____
_____
_____
_____
_____

Extreme Success: 90 DAY Devotional Journal

What is blocking your success in achieving this?

_____
_____
_____
_____
_____
_____
_____

Consider one or two steps of implementing your success:

_____
_____
_____
_____
_____
_____
_____

Find scriptures to support your success today:

_____
_____
_____
_____
_____
_____
_____

EXTREME THOUGHT: DAY 84

Stand bold and courageous, not wavering, ever-abounding, unmovable, unshakable, determined, strong, unbeatable, undefeatable, powerhouse in Jesus. Stand! Stand!

(Post this on your social media.)

What thoughts come to mind when you read the above statement?

_____
_____
_____
_____
_____
_____

Where are you today? Are you successful in this? Why or why not?

_____
_____
_____
_____
_____
_____

Extreme Success: 90 DAY Devotional Journal

What is blocking your success in achieving this?

_____
_____
_____
_____
_____
_____
_____

Consider one or two steps of implementing your success:

_____
_____
_____
_____
_____
_____
_____

Find scriptures to support your success today:

_____
_____
_____
_____
_____
_____
_____

EXTREME THOUGHT: DAY 85

Strengthen your faith by weight lifting the Bible from off the table and into your arms, up to your face, then down again. Then, exercise your legs by getting down on the floor for prayer and back up! Look at those muscles!
(Actually, pick up your Bible from off the table. Lift it up and begin to read. After you read, get down on your knees and pray)

What thoughts come to mind when you read the above statement?

_____
_____
_____
_____
_____
_____
_____

Where are you today? Are you successful in this?
Why or why not?

_____
_____
_____
_____
_____
_____

Extreme Success: 90 DAY Devotional Journal

What is blocking your success in achieving this?

_____
_____
_____
_____
_____
_____

Consider one or two steps of implementing your success:

_____
_____
_____
_____
_____
_____

Find scriptures to support your success today:

_____
_____
_____
_____
_____
_____

EXTREME THOUGHT: DAY 86

Run your race with passion and fire in your heart. Your fire in Jesus is unquenchable. It can not be extinguished. Your fire is getting hotter and hotter! Burn baby burn!

(Write on a note and say, "burn baby burn" and place it on your mirror.)

What thoughts come to mind when you read the above statement?

_____
_____
_____
_____
_____
_____
_____

Where are you today? Are you successful in this? Why or why not?

_____
_____
_____
_____
_____
_____
_____

Extreme Success: 90 DAY Devotional Journal

What is blocking your success in achieving this?

_____
_____
_____
_____
_____
_____

Consider one or two steps of implementing your success:

_____
_____
_____
_____
_____
_____

Find scriptures to support your success today:

_____
_____
_____
_____
_____
_____

EXTREME THOUGHT: DAY 87

Seek! Run! Strive! Desire! Want! Hunger! Thirst! Pant and crave for the presence of God! Rush into His secret place and refuse to come out! You'll be protected there forever.

(Play the song by Micah Stampley, "I'm in another place".)

What thoughts come to mind when you read the above statement?

_____
_____
_____
_____
_____
_____
_____

Where are you today? Are you successful in this? Why or why not?

_____
_____
_____
_____
_____
_____

Extreme Success: 90 DAY Devotional Journal

What is blocking your success in achieving this?

_____
_____
_____
_____
_____
_____
_____

Consider one or two steps of implementing your success:

_____
_____
_____
_____
_____
_____
_____

Find scriptures to support your success today:

_____
_____
_____
_____
_____
_____
_____

EXTREME THOUGHT: DAY 88

Faith is when God decides not to heal, deliver nor touch you but you still believe He can and will. Faith is when God says "no", but you still trust he made the right decision!

What thoughts come to mind when you read the above statement?

_____
_____
_____
_____
_____
_____
_____

Where are you today? Are you successful in this? Why or why not?

_____
_____
_____
_____
_____
_____
_____

Extreme Success: 90 DAY Devotional Journal

What is blocking your success in achieving this?

_____
_____
_____
_____
_____
_____
_____

Consider one or two steps of implementing your success:

_____
_____
_____
_____
_____
_____
_____

Find scriptures to support your success today:

_____
_____
_____
_____
_____
_____
_____

EXTREME THOUGHT: DAY 89

When God speaks to us, we seek confirmation. When the enemy speaks his lies about us, do we believe him the first time? Believe in God's Word the FIRST TIME He speaks!

(Say to the Lord, "help me to believe You the first time that You speak".)

What thoughts come to mind when you read the above statement?

_____
_____
_____
_____
_____
_____

Where are you today? Are you successful in this? Why or why not?

_____
_____
_____
_____
_____
_____

Extreme Success: 90 DAY Devotional Journal

What is blocking your success in achieving this?

_____
_____
_____
_____
_____
_____
_____

Consider one or two steps of implementing your success:

_____
_____
_____
_____
_____
_____
_____

Find scriptures to support your success today:

_____
_____
_____
_____
_____
_____
_____

EXTREME THOUGHT: DAY 90

Brace yourself for the next big move of God which may blow your mind. The people who truly seek the face of God will be flowing in this move. If that's not you, your sins may be exposed, and you will be left wondering what happened. Hidden agendas, NO MORE! Your move is here.

(Review the last 90 days and see your progress. Share this book with other.)

What thoughts come to mind when you read the above statement?

_____
_____
_____
_____
_____
_____
_____

Where are you today? Are you successful in this? Why or why not?

_____
_____
_____
_____
_____
_____

Made in the USA
Coppell, TX
22 July 2021